HUMAN ENLIGHTENMENT

For forty years Sangharakshita has been playing an important part in the spread of Buddhism throughout the modern world. He is head of the Western Buddhist Order (Trailokya Bauddha Mahasangha), and is actively engaged in what is now an international Buddhist movement with centres in thirteen countries worldwide. When not visiting centres he is based at a community in Norfolk. His writings are available in eleven languages.

Also by Sangharakshita:
A Survey of Buddhism
Flame in Darkness
The Enchanted Heart
The Three Jewels
Crossing the Stream
The Essence of Zen
The Thousand-Petalled Lotus
The Religion of Art
The Ten Pillars of Buddhism
The Eternal Legacy
Travel Letters
Alternative Traditions
Conquering New Worlds
Ambedkar and Buddhism
The History of My Going for Refuge
The Taste of Freedom
Hercules and the Birds and Other Poems
New Currents in Western Buddhism
A Guide to the Buddhist Path
Learning to Walk
Vision and Transformation
The Buddha's Victory
Facing Mount Kanchenjunga
The FWBO and 'Protestant Buddhism'
The Drama of Cosmic Enlightenment

The Meaning of Orthodoxy in Buddhism
Mind—Reactive and Creative
Aspects of Buddhist Morality
Buddhism and Blasphemy
Buddhism, World Peace, and Nuclear War
The Bodhisattva: Evolution and Self-Transcendence
The Glory of the Literary World
Going For Refuge
The Caves of Bhaja
My Relation to the Order
Buddhism and the West

SANGHARAKSHITA

HUMAN ENLIGHTENMENT

AN ENCOUNTER WITH THE
IDEALS AND METHODS OF BUDDHISM

WINDHORSE PUBLICATIONS

Published by Windhorse Publications
T/L, 3 Sanda Street
Glasgow G20 8PU

Printed by The Cromwell Press,
Melksham, Wiltshire

British Library Cataloguing in Publication Data.
A catalogue record for this book is available from the British Library

Cover design Dhammarati
The cover shows Padmasambhava as Guru Shakya Senge,
courtesy of Clear Vision

Publisher's note: Since this work is intended for a general readership,
Pali and Sanskrit words have been transliterated without the diacritical marks
which would have been approporiate in a work of a more scholarly nature.

ISBN 0 904766 57 8
(ISBN 0 904766 30 6 second edition)

CONTENTS

To all the Upasakas, Upasikas,
Mitras, and Friends
with whom I shared
the experience of Spiritual Community
on my two visits
to the Land of the Long White Cloud

Preface

THE IDEAL OF HUMAN ENLIGHTENMENT is the highest ideal conceivable by man. The way *par excellence* to the realization of that Ideal is meditation, understood as comprising all those methods that raise the level of consciousness and transform human life by acting directly on the mind itself. Like all other methods of raising the level of consciousness—all other ways of realizing the Ideal of Human Enlightenment—meditation is best practised within the context of the Spiritual Community, that is to say, within the context of a free association of true individuals who are united in their common commitment to a common goal and who relate to one another primarily on that basis. It is with these related themes of Enlightenment, meditation, and spiritual community that the three lectures that make up the present volume are concerned.

The lectures were given in the Town Hall, Auckland, on 6, 13, and 20 February 1975, under the auspices of The Friends of the Western Buddhist Order (FWBO). I had arrived in New Zealand three months earlier, and in the course of that time had conducted meditation classes at the FWBO centres in Auckland and Christchurch, besides leading retreats in various places. FWBO activities had started in New Zealand as long ago as 1970–71, when Dharmachari Akshobhya started holding meditation classes in Auckland and Lim Poi Cheng began playing the tapes of my lectures in Christchurch. Now, four or five years later, the movement had gathered sufficient momentum for nine or ten people to want to commit themselves to the Three Jewels—to the Buddha, the Dharma, and the Sangha—as Dharmachari *(masc.)* and Dharmacharini *(fem.)* members of the Western Buddhist Order, and it was largely in response to their request that I had decided to visit New Zealand. The first batch of ordinations had, in fact, been held two months earlier, so that when I gave my lectures there was already a presence of the Order in New Zealand and thus, it was hoped, a firm basis for the future development of the movement in that country.

During the time I was giving the lectures I stayed outside Auckland, in the Waitakere Hills. All around me were slopes covered with the vivid green of what I had come to recognize as typical New Zealand bush. It was bush that was resonant with the chirring of cicadas and with unfamiliar bird-calls, and from which the opossums came out at night. Shortly before the lectures began, a friend brought me a copy of the poster that had been printed. Looking at it, I noticed that the lectures had been announced not as lectures on Buddhism but as *Buddhist* lectures. Whether intentional or not, the emphasis was significant. Buddhism is not a 'subject', not a body of facts on which one can talk without being involved in the meaning of those facts, and my lectures were therefore not lectures on Buddhism in the same sense that one might have lectures on Botany or Biology. The lectures that I gave in Auckland were *Buddhist* lectures, and as such they were meant not merely to convey facts about Buddhism, whether historical or doctrinal, but rather to communicate the results of one individual Buddhist's personal experience of Buddhism, in both East and West, over a period of more than thirty years.

Although my involvement with classes, retreats, and lectures did not allow me to see as much of New Zealand as I would have liked, I saw enough of it to convince me that conditions there were as favourable to the leading of the spiritual life as they were anywhere in the world—perhaps even more favourable. New Zealand had an agreeable climate and great natural beauty. Life under its blue skies was comparatively relaxed, and it was not difficult to make a living. Even in a place like Auckland there was not much hurry and bustle, not much pressure. There was plenty of space—plenty of fresh air—for everybody. Indeed, in a country somewhat bigger than Great Britain there were only three million people, nearly two thirds of them concentrated in the three major cities. Moreover, the country as a whole was relatively free from internal tensions, and people were not particularly weighed down by social convention and religious tradition. I therefore felt that the Path of the Higher Evolution, as I had outlined it in my three Buddhist lectures, had a great future in New Zealand, *if only people made the effort to practise it*—if only they took full advantage of the facilities for spiritual self-development that were being increasingly offered by the FWBO. This feeling was confirmed on my second visit, which took place in 1979. Even in those parts of the world where conditions were *not* so favourable to the spiritual life as they are in New Zealand, it is of course still possible to follow the Path of the Higher Evolution—still possible to realize the Ideal of Human Enlightenment—and it is for this reason that these lectures are now being brought out in book form, in the hope that in this form they will be able to reach a wider audience than the one to which the 'Ideal of Human Enlightenment' was originally presented.

I would like to thank Dharmachari Nagabodhi and Nigel Seller for their work in editing the verbatim transcript of these lectures for publication.

Sangharakshita
Padmaloka
Surlingham
Norfolk
28 May 1980

THE IDEAL OF HUMAN ENLIGHTENMENT

WHEN A BUDDHIST THINKS about Buddhism—about what Buddhists call the Dharma—usually the first thing of which he thinks is the Buddha, 'the Enlightened One'. Strangely enough, the first thing of which the non-Buddhist too usually thinks is the Buddha. We may not know anything at all about the teachings of Buddhism, but we will at least have seen an image or picture of the Buddha, and may even be quite familiar with it, even have a definite feeling for it. What, then, does that image or picture show? It shows a man in the prime of life, well built and handsome. He is seated cross-legged beneath a tree. His eyes are half closed and there is a smile on his lips. Looking at the figure we feel that, as a whole, it conveys an impression of solidity and stability, as well as of strength. It conveys an impression of absolute calm, absolute repose. But what attracts us most of all, more even than the total figure itself, is the face, because this conveys something which it is very difficult indeed to put into words. As we look at it, perhaps even concentrate on it, we see that the face is alive, that it is *alight*, and in that light we see reflected an unfathomable knowledge, a boundless compassion, and an ineffable joy. This, then, is the figure, this the image or the picture, of the Buddha, the Enlightened One. Usually it represents the historical Gautama the Buddha, the 'founder' of Buddhism, represents, that is to say, the great Indian teacher who lived approximately five hundred years before Jesus of Nazareth. But the figure also possesses a wider significance. It represents the subject of this lecture. In other words, it represents *The Ideal of Human Enlightenment*.

Human Enlightenment is the central theme, the central preoccupation, of Buddhism. It is what Buddhism is basically concerned with, both theoretically and practically. Indeed, it is what the Buddhist himself is basically concerned with. In the course of this lecture, therefore, we shall be trying to understand what is meant by Enlightenment in general and, in particular, by 'Human Enlightenment'.

Before going into this subject, however, I want to say a few words about the third item in our title. I want to examine the word 'ideal'. We speak of 'The *Ideal* of Human Enlightenment', but what does the word mean? I do not want to go into the dictionary definitions, much less still into what are really philosophical questions. For the purpose of our present discussion we shall confine ourselves to the ordinary, everyday usage of the word.

In the first place, the word means 'the best imaginable of its kind'. For instance, in London, every summer, there is a famous exhibition known as the Ideal Home Exhibition. Every year thousands, even hundreds of thousands, of people visit it and look around the different sections.

There they see ideal kitchens, ideal bathrooms, ideal garages, ideal shaving mirrors, ideal bread knives, ideal refrigerators, ideal lawnmowers, ideal armchairs, and even ideal egg-whisks! They see hundreds of different items, each of them claiming to be 'ideal', the best imaginable of its kind (though, of course, different manufacturers may have different ideas as to what actually is the 'best'). Each of them, it is claimed, fulfils its function in the best possible way, and all of these things add up to the 'ideal home', add up, in other words, to the best imaginable home, the home that perfectly fulfils the function of a home, the home that everybody would like to live in—if only they could afford it.

In the same way we speak of various other things. We speak of the ideal wife, which is to say the wife who is a good cook and manager, who keeps the ideal home in perfect order, who drives her husband to work every morning, who never asks him for extra housekeeping money, and who laughs at all his jokes. We even speak of the ideal husband, though he is of course much rarer. Similarly we speak of the ideal couple, the ideal holiday, ideal weather, ideal arrangements, the ideal job, the ideal employer, the ideal employee, and so on. In other words we speak of something as being the best imaginable of its kind, as best fulfilling its natural function or what is believed to be its natural function. This is the first usage of the term.

In the second place, the word 'ideal' means a model or pattern: something that can be taken as an example, and imitated or copied. Nowadays this usage is less common than the first, although it overlaps it to some extent. According to this usage, we see that the ideal home is not merely the best imaginable home but also the model, or pattern, for all homes. It is what you should try to make your own home look like, at least to some extent. Thus this usage would suggest that the ideal is a model. It implies a sort of comparison between the ideal, on the one hand, and the actual on the other, in this case between the real home that we actually have and the ideal home that we would like to have if we could afford it.

There is, however, a third usage of the term. For example, suppose you ask a friend what he would like to do when he retires. He might say that what he would really like to do is go away to some beautiful tropical island with a marvellous climate, with beautiful sunshine, beautiful beaches, beautiful sea, beautiful surf, and just live there for the rest of his life, just to get away from it all. But then perhaps he says, 'Ah well, I don't suppose I ever shall. It's just an ideal.' In this instance the word 'ideal' represents a state of affairs that is regarded as highly desirable, which is certainly imaginable—which you can certainly conceive, even quite clearly—but which is regarded, for some reason or other, as impossible of attainment. These, then, are the three different ways in which we use the word 'ideal'.

Having gained some understanding of how we use the word 'ideal', we come on to a very important question, and with this question we start to approach the heart of our present subject. We have spoken of the ideal home, and we can all understand what that might be. We have mentioned the ideal wife, the ideal husband, the ideal job—even the ideal egg-whisk. But we have forgotten perhaps one thing. What about the person who uses all these articles, who enters into all these relationships?

What about the individual human being? We seem to have lost sight of him, or of her—as so easily happens in the midst of the complexities of modern life. The question that we are really asking is 'What is the ideal man?' We all think we know what is meant by the ideal home, the ideal wife, or the ideal husband, but have we ever considered the question, 'What is the best imaginable kind of human being?' Not just the best kind of employee, or the best kind of citizen, or the best kind of member of a particular social group, or a particular age group, but the best kind of man *per se*, the best kind of man *as man*. Because we *are* men, and this question very seriously concerns us. What *is* the ideal for our lives? The Buddhist answer to this question comes clearly, categorically, and unambiguously. The ideal man is the Enlightened man. The ideal man is the Buddha. That is to say, the ideal for humanity—the ideal for individual human beings—is Enlightenment. The ideal is Buddhahood.

Now this raises three questions, and with each question we have to deal in turn. The three questions are, firstly, 'What is Enlightenment, or Buddhahood?' Secondly, 'How do we know that this state which we call Enlightenment is the ideal for man?' Thirdly, 'Where does this ideal of Enlightenment come from? Whence do we derive it? Whence does it originate?' Once these three questions are answered we shall have, perhaps, quite a good idea—or at least a general idea—of what is meant by 'The Ideal of Human Enlightenment'.

Buddhist tradition, of all schools, speaks of Enlightenment as comprising mainly three things. To begin with, Enlightenment is spoken of as a state of pure, clear—even radiant—awareness. Some schools go so far as to say that in this state of awareness the subject–object duality is no longer experienced. There is no 'out there', no 'in here'. That distinction, that subject–object distinction as we usually call it, is entirely transcended. There is only one continuous, pure, clear awareness, extending as it were in all directions, pure and homogeneous. It is, moreover, an awareness of things *as they really are*, which is, of course, not things in the sense of objects, but things as, so to speak, transcending the duality of subject and object. Hence this pure, clear awareness is also spoken of as an awareness of Reality, and therefore also as a state of knowledge. This knowledge is not knowledge in the ordinary sense—not the knowledge which functions within the framework of the subject–object duality—but rather a state of direct, unmediated spiritual vision that sees all things directly, clearly, vividly, and truly. It is a spiritual vision—even a transcendental vision—which is free from all delusion, all misconception, all wrong, crooked thinking, all vagueness, all obscurity, all mental conditioning, all prejudice. First of all, then, Enlightenment is this state of pure, clear awareness, this state of knowledge or vision. Secondly, and no less importantly, Enlightenment is spoken of as a state of intense, profound, overflowing love and compassion. Sometimes this love is compared to the love of a mother for her only child. This comparison occurs, for instance, in a very famous Buddhist text called the *Metta*

Sutta, the 'Discourse of Loving Kindness'. In this discourse the Buddha says 'Just as a mother protects her only son even at the cost of her own life, so should one develop a mind of all-embracing love towards all living beings.' This is the sort of feeling, the sort of attitude, that we must cultivate. You notice that the Buddha does not just talk about all human beings, but all *living* beings: all that lives, all that breathes, all that moves, all that is sentient. This is how the Enlightened mind feels. And that love and compassion consists, we are further told, in a heartfelt desire— a deep, burning desire—for their well-being, for their happiness: a desire that all beings should be set free from suffering, from all difficulties, that they should grow and develop, and that ultimately they should gain Enlightenment. Love and compassion of this kind—love infinite, overflowing, boundless, directed towards all living beings—this too is part of Enlightenment.

Thirdly, Enlightenment consists in a state, or experience, of inexhaustible mental and spiritual energy. We see this very well exemplified by an incident in the life of the Buddha himself. As you may know, he gained Enlightenment at the age of thirty-five, and he continued teaching and communicating with others until the ripe old age of eighty, although his physical body eventually became very frail. On one occasion he said 'My body is just like an old, broken-down cart, which has been repaired many times. It has been kept going with bits of string, as it were. But my mind is as vigorous as ever. Even if I had to be carried from place to place on a litter, if anyone came to me, I would still be able to answer his questions, I would still be able to teach him. My intellectual and spiritual vigour is undiminished, despite the enfeebled state of my body.' So energy is characteristic of the state of Enlightenment. We could say that the state of Enlightenment is one of tremendous energy, of absolute spontaneity, continually bubbling forth: a state of uninterrupted creativity. In a nutshell, we may say that the state of Enlightenment is a state of perfect, unconditioned freedom from all subjective limitations.

This, then, is what is meant by Enlightenment, as it is understood in the Buddhist tradition—so far, at least, as Enlightenment can be described, so far as its different aspects can be tabulated in this way. What really happens is that knowledge passes into love and compassion, love and compassion into energy, energy into knowledge, and so on. We cannot really split any one aspect off from the others. Nonetheless, we are traditionally given this 'tabulated' account of Enlightenment, just to convey some hint of the experience, just to give some little idea, or feeling, of what it is like. If we want to have a better idea than this, then we shall have to read, perhaps, some more extended, poetic account, preferably one found in the Buddhist scriptures; or we shall have to take up the practice of meditation, and try to get at least a glimpse of the state of Enlightenment as we meditate. So when Buddhism speaks of Enlightenment, of Buddhahood or nirvana, this is what it means: it means a state of supreme knowledge, love and compassion, and energy.

How Do We Know That This State of Enlightenment is The Ideal For Man?

Before attempting to answer this question, we shall have to distinguish between two kinds of ideal. There are no actual terms for them in circulation, but we can call them 'natural ideals' and 'artificial ideals'. A natural ideal, we may say, is an ideal which takes into consideration the nature of the thing or the person for which it is an ideal. The artificial ideal, on the other hand, does not do this. The artificial ideal imposes itself from the outside, in an artificial manner. For instance, if we go back to our ideal home, then however beautiful, however luxurious, however convenient it may be in many ways, it would not be an ideal home for a crippled person if it contained several flights of steep stairs. In the same way the life of a Henry Ford would not be an ideal for someone who was, by temperament, an artist.

Using this distinction, we may say that Enlightenment is not an artificial ideal. It is not something imposed on man from outside, something that does not belong to him or accord with his nature. Enlightenment is a natural ideal for man, or even, we may say, *the* natural ideal. There is nothing artificial about it, nothing arbitrary. It is an ideal that corresponds to man's nature, and to his needs. We know this in two ways. I have spoken about the nature of Enlightenment, and obviously it has seemed, though intelligible, something very, very rarified indeed, something very remote, even, from our present experience. But the qualities that constitute Enlightenment are, in fact, already found in man, in germinal form. They are not completely foreign to him. They are, in a sense, natural to man. In every man, in every woman, and even in every child, there is *some* knowledge—*some* experience—of Reality, however remote and far removed, *some* feeling of love and compassion, however limited and exclusive, and *some* energy, however gross and unrefined, however conditioned and unspontaneous. All these qualities are already there, to some extent. It is, in fact, these qualities that distinguish man from the animal. But in the state of Enlightenment these qualities are fully and perfectly developed, to a degree that we can hardly imagine. It is for this reason— because the qualities of knowledge, love, and energy are already present within him, in however embryonic a form—that man has, as it were, a natural affinity with Enlightenment, and can respond to the ideal of Enlightenment when he encounters it. Thus even when someone speaks in terms of absolute knowledge, of the vision of Reality, or in terms of boundless, unlimited love and compassion for all living beings, it is not something completely foreign to us, it is not just so many words. We *can* feel something. And this is because the germ, the seed, is already there, in our own experience, and we can respond to the ideal of Enlightenment whenever and however we encounter it—even when we encounter it in comparatively weak, limited, or distorted forms.

We also know that Enlightenment is the natural ideal for man because, in the long run, man is never really satisfied by anything else. We can have all sorts of pleasures, all sorts of achievements, but eventually we still feel within ourselves something dissatisfied, something non-satisfied. This is what in Buddhism is called *dukkha*: unsatisfactoriness, or even suffering. Tradition speaks of three forms of *dukkha*, three kinds of suffering. The first is called simply 'the suffering which is suffering'. It is obviously suffering if we cut our finger, or when someone upsets us or disappoints us, for instance. This is the kind of suffering that is, simply, suffering. Then there is what is called 'suffering by way of transformation'. We have something,

we enjoy it—we get a great deal of pleasure from it—but
by its very nature that thing cannot last, or our relationship with it cannot last. Eventually the thing goes, the
relationship with it breaks up, and because we have en-
joyed it, because we have become very attached to it,
suffering results. This is the suffering that comes about as
a result of transformation, of change, of time. Then there
is 'the suffering of conditioned existence itself': the suffering, ultimately, of everything which is not Enlightenment.
Even if we do acquire things, and even if we go on pos-
sessing them and enjoying them, there is still some corner
of our heart which is not satisfied, which wants something
more, something further, something greater. And this
something is what we call Enlightenment. So from this too
we know that Enlightenment is the natural ideal for man,
because man, the true man, the real human being, the true
Individual, ultimately is not satisfied with anything less.
Personifying the ideal of Enlightenment, and borrowing
the somewhat theistic language of St Augustine, we may
say, 'Thou hast made us for thyself, and our hearts are
restless until they find rest in thee.'

WHERE DOES THE IDEAL OF ENLIGHTENMENT COME FROM?

The ideal comes from human life itself; it comes from
human history. It could not come from any other source.
The ideal for man, we may say, can only come from man
himself, can only come from a human being. And if we
look back into history we can see various people who have
actually achieved Enlightenment, who have closed the
gap between the real and the ideal. We can see people who
have fully actualized all those spiritual qualities which in

most men and women are only germinal. If we look back in history we can see individuals who are living embodiments of the ideal. In particular, as we look back into the history of the East, of India, we see the figure of the Buddha. We see the figure of the young Indian patrician who, some 2,500 years ago, gained Enlightenment or, as the Buddhist scriptures call it, *bodhi*, which is 'knowledge', or 'awakening'. He it was who, after gaining that state of Enlightenment, inaugurated the great spiritual revolution—the great spiritual tradition—that we now call Buddhism.

At this point I would like to clear up certain misunderstandings that exist with regard to the Buddha and Buddhism. At the beginning of this lecture I said that even the non-Buddhist has at least seen an image or picture of the Buddha, and that he might even be quite familiar with it. However, although he might have seen it many times, he may not have a very clear idea of what it represents; he may not know who, or what, the Buddha is. There are, in fact, on the part of many people, some quite serious misunderstandings about him. There are in particular two major misunderstandings: firstly that the Buddha was an ordinary man, and secondly that the Buddha was God. Both of these misunderstandings are the result of thinking, consciously or unconsciously, in Christian terms, or at least in theistic terms, which is to say, in terms of a personal God, a supreme being who has created the universe, and who governs it by his providence.

For orthodox Christianity, as most of us know, God and man are entirely different beings. God is 'up there', man is 'down here', and there is a great gulf between them. God is the creator. He has called man into existence, out of the dust. Man is the created. He has been created, according to some accounts, much as a potter creates a pot. Moreover, God is pure, God is holy, God is sinless; but man is sinful, and man can never become God: such an idea would be meaningless according to orthodox Christian, theistic tradition. Not only that. With only one exception, God can never become man. The exception is, of course, Jesus Christ, who for orthodox Christianity is God incarnate. Thus the Christian has, we may say, three categories with which to operate: God, man—which is to say 'sinful man', and God incarnate, or 'Christ'. So where does the Buddha fit in? How does the orthodox Christian apply his categories when confronted by the figure of the Buddha? Obviously for the orthodox Christian the Buddha is not God. (There is only one God anyway.) Equally obviously, he is not God incarnate, since according to orthodox Christian teaching God incarnated only once, as Jesus Christ. That leaves only man. Orthodox Christians, therefore, when confronted by the figure of the Buddha, classify him as a man—as an ordinary man, essentially just like everyone else—even as a sinful man albeit perhaps better than most people. But however much better he might be, he is still seen as immeasurably inferior to God, and immeasurably inferior to Christ.

So much then for the first misunderstanding. The second arises out of the first. It is said, even by Christian scholars working in the field of Buddhist studies, that although the Buddha was only an ordinary man his followers made him into a God. You often read in books, even now, that after his death the Buddha's followers 'deified' him. This is indicated, we are told, by the fact that Buddhists *worship* the Buddha, and of course worship is due only to God. If you worship someone or something, a Christian will inevitably think that you are treating it, or him, as God.

Now both these misunderstandings can be cleared up quite easily. All we have to do is to free ourselves from our Christian conditioning, a conditioning which affects—at least unconsciously—even those who no longer think of themselves as Christians. We have to stop trying to think of the Buddha in what are really non-Buddhistic terms. We have to remember that Buddhism is a non-theistic tradition—which is to say that it does not believe in the existence of a supreme being who created the universe. Buddhism, in fact, distinctly denies the existence of such a being. The Buddha even went so far as to treat the belief in a personal God, a creator figure, as a hindrance to the living of the spiritual life.

So who, or what, was the Buddha? How do *Buddhists* think of him? How did he think of himself? In the first place, the Buddha was a man, a human being. But he was not an ordinary man. He was an Enlightened man: a man who was the living embodiment of perfect knowledge, unbounded love and compassion, and inexhaustible energy. But he was not *born* an extraordinary man. He *became* an extraordinary man, became an Enlightened One, as a result of his own human effort to make actual what was potential in himself, to develop to the full what was only germinal in himself. So Buddhism recognizes two great categories: the category of the ordinary man, and the category of the Enlightened man. Now, although the gulf between these two is not unbridgeable, as is the gulf between God and man in Christianity, the distance between them is very, very great, and it takes a tremendous effort to traverse this gap. Many Buddhists, in fact, believe that this effort has to be maintained through a whole succession of lives, whether here on earth or in higher realms. For this reason, the Enlightened man is regarded as constituting an independent category of existence. According to Buddhism, the Enlightened man is regarded as the highest being in the universe, higher even than the gods. For this reason the Enlightened man is worshipped. He is worshipped out of gratitude for setting an example, for showing the way, for showing us what we too are capable of becoming. In other words, the Buddha is worshipped not as God, but as Teacher, as Exemplar, as Guide.

In this connection, Gautama the Buddha is often referred to as *Lokajyestha*. In the West Gautama the Buddha is best known simply as the Buddha, but in the East there are quite a few well-known titles for him. He is known as *Tathagata*, as *Bhagavan*, as *Arahat*, and also as *Lokajyestha*. The term *Lokajyestha* means 'the elder brother of the world', or 'elder brother of mankind', and the Buddha is so called because he has been born, spiritually, first, as we are born, spiritually, afterwards. The Buddha is often represented as saying to his disciples 'You are my own true sons, born of my mouth, born of the Teaching: the heirs to spiritual things, not heirs to worldly things.' Sometimes, as in the *Vinaya Pitaka*, the Buddha is compared to the first chick to emerge from a clutch of eggs. The first-born chick starts to tap on the shells of the other eggs with his little beak, helping the other chicks to emerge. And so, we are told, the Buddha is like that first chick. He is the first to emerge from the shell of ignorance, the shell of spiritual darkness and blindness, and then he taps on our shells, he wakes us up with his Teaching—he helps us to *emerge*.

From all this we can see that the Buddhist conception of the Enlightened man, the Buddha, represents a category for which we have no equivalent in Western thought or Western religious tradition. He is neither God nor man in the Christian sense. He is not even man-without-God—man left on his own without God, as it were. He is something in between and above.

Perhaps we can best think of Enlightened man in evolutionary terms. Man is an animal, but he is no ordinary animal. For want of a better term, he is a rational animal. He represents a new mutation, a new species, a new category: an animal but, at the same time, infinitely more than an animal. He is a human being, a man. In the same way, a Buddha is a man, but he is not an ordinary man. He is an Enlightened man. He too represents a new mutation, a new species, a new category of existence: a human being but, at the same time, infinitely more than a human being: an *Enlightened* human being, a *Buddha*.

We can now move on to the misunderstandings about Buddhism. These are, as one might expect, closely connected with the misunderstandings about the Buddha. Inasmuch as Buddhism is non-theistic, it is not really a religion in the ordinary Western sense of the term. People sometimes find this hard to understand because they have always regarded Buddhism as a religion. Perhaps they have seen it classified in this way in encyclopaedias, or on television, or of course they have a vague idea that 'religion' means belief in God anyway. They therefore think that Buddhism *must* teach belief in God. But this is just muddled thinking. Some people even think there must be a God in Buddhism *somewhere*—and do their best to find him. They even accuse Buddhists of mislaying him, or losing him, or even trying to hide him!

If Buddhism is not a religion in the Christian sense, then what is it? We can best answer this question by going back to our distinction between the real and the ideal, between the Enlightened man and the unenlightened man. Buddhism, or what is traditionally known as the Dharma, is whatever helps us transform the real into the ideal. It is whatever helps us to bridge the gap between the state of ignorance and the state of Enlightenment. In other words, Buddhism is whatever helps us to develop, whatever helps us to grow. For this reason we find the Buddha saying to his aunt and foster mother, Mahaprajapati Gautami, 'Whatsoever teachings conduce to dispassion, to detachment, to decrease of worldly gains, to frugality, to content, to solitude, to energy, to delight in good, of these teachings you can be certain that they are the Teaching of the Buddha.' The criterion is, then, not theoretical but practical. In the course of its long history, Buddhism has developed many different philosophies, as we may call them, many different methods, many different institutions, but they all have one sole purpose, and that purpose is to assist the individual human being to develop from the state of an ordinary human being to the state of an Enlightened human being, a Buddha.

Let us conclude, then, as we began: with the figure of Gautama the Buddha. He is seated under the bodhi tree, just a few weeks after his great awakening. According to one of the oldest accounts, at that time he looked out over the world, over the whole of humanity—not with the eye of the flesh but with his spiritual vision, or what is called his 'divine eye'. And as he looked out in this way, he saw mankind as like a great bed of lotus flowers. He saw, moreover, that some of the flowers were deeply immersed in the mud, while others rose half out of the water. Some were even standing completely clear of the water. In other words, he saw all these 'flowers'—all human beings—as being at different stages of growth, different stages of development. And that, we could say, is how Buddhism has seen humanity ever since: as a bed of plants capable of producing shoots, as shoots capable of producing buds, as buds capable of opening into flowers, into lotus flowers, even into the thousand-petalled lotus itself. But in order to grow, in order to develop, human beings must have something to grow *into*. They cannot grow unconsciously, as the plant does: they must grow consciously. We may say, in fact, that for human beings growth *means* growth in consciousness, growth in awareness. This is why man needs an ideal—not just an ideal for this or that aspect of his being only, not an ideal for himself simply in terms of this or that relationship of life, but an ideal for himself as a human being. It must be an ideal, moreover, which is not artificial but natural, not imposed upon him from without but implicit in his own nature, his own being: an ideal which represents, indeed, the fulfilment of his nature in the deepest possible sense. It is this ideal, the ideal of human Enlightenment, that I have tried to communicate to you in this lecture.

Nowadays we have to recognize that many people are sceptical about ideals, and especially so, perhaps, about spiritual ideals—about the possibility of transforming the real into the ideal. Buddhism, however, is not sceptical. It has faith in the ideal—faith in the spiritual ideal, faith in the ideal of human Enlightenment—and it has faith in the ideal because it has faith in man, in the creative potential of man. Because it has faith in man, it asks man to have faith in himself. It does not ask him to 'believe', least of all to 'believe' in Buddhism. Instead, it asks him to take the ideal of human Enlightenment as a practical, working hypothesis. It asks him to *make the experiment*. It asks him to *try*.

What Meditation Really Is

In the course of the last few decades quite a number of changes have taken place in different parts of the world, particularly, perhaps, in the Western world. Political changes have taken place, as well as social changes, cultural changes, and also great technological changes. We might even go so far as to say that in the course of the last few decades more changes have taken place in the world, and in the Western world in particular, than during any comparable period in human history.

So far as human affairs, at least, are concerned, in the course of the last decade or more we have seen a constantly accelerating rate of change. More and more changes seem to be taking place, within shorter and ever shorter periods of time. Formerly, when the pace was slower, and you had time to 'grow up', several generations might elapse before a change in some particular department of life started becoming noticeable. But this is no longer the case. Now these changes are noticeable in the course of a single lifetime, even in the space of a single decade—or half a decade. And we see this constantly accelerating rate of change in practically all fields of human life and human endeavour, whether political, social, economic, or cultural.

But in this lecture we are concerned with just one of those fields, which I shall call—to use a good, neutral, general term—the cultural field. In this particular field, one of the biggest, one of the greatest, and also potentially one of the most important changes to have taken place in recent years is with regard to the subject of meditation.

Fifteen or twenty years ago, meditation had hardly been heard of in the West. Whatever knowledge or interest there was, so far as meditation was concerned, was for the most part confined to obscure groups and eccentric individuals. But now we may say that the term meditation is almost a household word. Nevertheless, although the word is widely current, this does not mean that what the word represents—what meditation *means*—is at all well understood.

So many times I have heard people say 'Meditation means making the mind a blank—making the mind empty.' Others seem to think that meditation simply means sitting and doing nothing. Sitting and doing nothing may be a fine thing to do, or not to do, but it is not meditation. Again, sometimes you hear people say, or you even read, that meditation means sitting and gazing at your navel, possibly squinting as you do so, or that it means 'going into some kind of trance'. (Unfortunately, one well-known and generally reliable writer on Buddhism has, to some extent, popularized this word 'trance' as a synonym for meditation.) Other people think that meditation means just sitting quietly and thinking about things, 'turning things over in one's mind'. Others again think that meditation means getting yourself into a sort of self-induced hypnotic state. These are just a few of the more popular and more widespread misunderstandings about meditation.

Why there should be these misunderstandings seems fairly obvious. Meditation is comparatively new in the West: at least it is new in the modern West. There has not been, at least in recent history, anything quite like it within the range of our experience. We do not even have the proper words, the proper specialized terms, to describe meditation states and meditation processes. It is only natural, therefore, that at first there should be some misunderstanding.

Again, we must remember that meditation is essentially something to be practised—that it is something which one does, or which one comes to experience. But most people still know about meditation only from hearsay. They do not know about it from their own personal practice and experience. They therefore rely on second hand, third hand, and even fourth hand information. Some even rely—perhaps have to rely—for their information about meditation on books. Nowadays there are quite a few books on the market dealing, or purporting to deal, with meditation. But unfortunately these books themselves are only too often based on hearsay, rather than on personal knowledge and experience. In some cases they may be based on pure imagination, not to say speculation. Already in this field there are quite a number of self-appointed experts. When something becomes popular, as meditation is becoming, only too many people are ready to cash in on the boom. I remember, in this connection, my own experience during the Buddha Jayanti year, the year in which the Buddhist world celebrated the 2,500th anniversary of the *parinirvana*, or passing away, of the Buddha—celebrated 2,500 years of Buddhism. The Government of India sponsored the celebrations in India, while the different south-east Asian governments sponsored the celebrations in their own respective countries. A great deal of interest was aroused, and since there was a great demand for literature all sorts of people set to work writing books, pamphlets, and articles on Buddhism, in many cases without the slightest qualification. There they were, all collecting material from here and there—sometimes from reliable, sometimes from unreliable, sources—and by this means all producing another 'work' on Buddhism.

In the West today there is a boom in spiritual things in general, and at least a modest boom in meditation. Quite a number of people are dissatisfied with their ordinary, everyday lives, their conventional way of living and doing things. People cannot accept a purely scientific explanation of life, despite the great practical success of science in dealing with the material world, while at the same time they find themselves unable to accept the traditional, mainly Judaeo–Christian, explanation of things either. They therefore begin looking for something which will satisfy them more deeply, more permanently, more creatively, and more constructively. Some people look in the direction of the Eastern spiritual traditions, and especially in the direction of meditation. They want to know about meditation, want to practise meditation—want to go along to meditation classes, attend meditation weekends—and in this way a demand for meditation is created.

Of course, only too many people are ready to fulfil that demand—in some cases for a consideration. Some of these people may be quite well qualified to meet the demand—quite well qualified to teach meditation—and others may not. In this way, too, all sorts of misunderstandings arise. Quite often meditation is identified with a particular *kind* of meditation, or with a particular concentration technique. It is not, perhaps, generally understood that there are many kinds of meditation—many methods—and many concentration techniques. Sometimes people who know about just one of these, or who practise just one, tend to identify the whole practice of meditation exclusively with that particular method, that particular technique. They may claim that their method is the best one, or even that it is the only one, and that you are not actually meditating at all unless you meditate in that particular way, using that particular technique. The other techniques, the other practices, the other traditions are, they claim, of no value. This is the sort of claim that is made. It becomes all the more important, therefore, to clear up the confusion, to resolve the misunderstandings. It becomes important to understand *what meditation really is*. In order to do this we shall have to bear in mind the gap between the ideal and the real, between the Enlightened man, or Buddha, and the unenlightened, ordinary man. We shall have to bear in mind the nature of Buddhism itself.

As we saw in the previous lecture, the Buddha, or Enlightened man, represents a state, an attainment—a mode of being and consciousness—for which we have really no equivalent in Western thought, and for which we have, therefore, no equivalent word or term. 'Buddha' does not mean God, the supreme being, the creator of the universe, nor does 'Buddha' mean God incarnate. Neither does 'Buddha' mean man, in the ordinary sense. Rather, we can best think of the Buddha, the Enlightened One, in evolutionary terms. The Buddha, the Enlightened One, is a man. But he is a very special kind of man, a more developed man. In fact he is an infinitely developed man. That is to say, he is a man who has reached, and realized fully, the state of spiritual perfection that we call Enlightenment. This is what 'Buddha' means. And Buddhism is whatever helps close the gap between the ideal and the real; whatever helps transform the unenlightened man into the Enlightened man; whatever helps us to grow, to evolve, to develop. When the real man becomes the ideal man— when the unenlightened man is transformed into the Enlightened man—a tremendous change takes place, perhaps the greatest human change and development that *can* take place. And it is this kind of development that we call the spiritual life, or the process of what is sometimes called the Higher Evolution. But what is it that changes? In what does this development consist?

Obviously it is not the physical body that changes, because physically the Enlightened man and the unenlightened man look very much alike. The change that takes place is a purely mental one—using the word mental in its widest sense. It is *consciousness* that develops. And this is the great difference, we may say, between the Higher Evolution, on the one hand, and the lower evolution, on the other. What we call the lower evolution corresponds to the whole process of development from amoeba up to ordinary man, or unenlightened man. This is

predominantly a biological process, a process that becomes psychological only towards the end. The Higher
Evolution corresponds to the whole process—the whole
course—of development which leads from unenlightened
man up to Enlightened man, and this is a purely psychological and spiritual process, a process which may, eventually, become entirely dissociated from the physical body.

Now traditional Buddhism speaks in terms of four
grades, or four levels, of consciousness, each one higher
than the one preceding. First of all there is consciousness
associated with the plane, or 'world', of sensuous experience. Secondly there is consciousness associated with
the plane, or 'world', of mental and spiritual form—the
plane or world of archetypes. Then there is consciousness
associated with the formless plane or 'world', and finally,
consciousness associated with the transcendental path,
which is to say, with the path leading directly to nirvana,
Enlightenment, or Buddhahood, as well as with nirvana,
Enlightenment, or Buddhahood itself.

There is another classification which we sometimes use,
which may be more helpful. Here too there are four stages,
or four levels, of consciousness, although they do not
correspond very exactly to the four already enumerated.
Here, first of all, comes what we call sense consciousness,
which is to say, consciousness associated with objects
experienced through the physical senses. This is sometimes called simple consciousness, also animal consciousness. It is the consciousness we share with members of the
animal kingdom. Secondly, there is self consciousness: not
self consciousness in the more colloquial sense of the term,
but self consciousness in the sense of *awareness of being
aware*, knowing that we know. This is sometimes called

reflexive consciousness because, here, consciousness so to speak bends back upon itself, knows itself, experiences itself, is aware of itself. We may say, perhaps, that this self consciousness, or reflexive consciousness, is human consciousness in the full sense of the term. Thirdly, there is what we call transcendental consciousness. This means consciousness of, or even direct personal contact with, Reality—ultimate Reality—experienced as an object 'out there'. Finally, there is absolute consciousness, in which the subject–object relation is entirely dissolved, and in which there is a full realization of ultimate Reality, as transcending altogether the subject–object duality.

In both these classifications, the first consciousness enumerated is that, predominantly, of the ordinary unenlightened man, the man who is not even trying to develop spiritually. And the fourth consciousness, in both cases, is that of the Enlightened man.

We can now begin to see in what the spiritual life—in what the Higher Evolution—essentially consists. We may say that it consists in a continual progression from lower to higher, and ever higher, states of being and consciousness: from the world of sensuous experience to the world of mental and spiritual form, from the world of mental and spiritual form to the formless world, and from the formless world to nirvana, or Enlightenment; or, from sense consciousness to self consciousness, self consciousness to transcendental consciousness, transcendental consciousness to absolute consciousness.

We can now begin to see what meditation really is. Indeed, we shall see it all the more clearly for having gone a little way into these fundamentals first. There is, however, just one more point to be made. Spiritual life, as we have said, consists in the development of consciousness. And Buddhism, the Dharma, the teaching of the Buddha, is whatever helps in that development. But there are two different ways in which consciousness can be developed, or at least two different methods of approach. We call these methods the subjective and the objective, or the direct and the indirect. Having recognized this distinction, we are at last in a position to see what meditation really is. Meditation is the subjective or direct way of raising the level of consciousness. In meditation we raise the level of consciousness by working directly on the mind itself.

First of all, however, I must say something about 'objective' or indirect methods of raising the level of consciousness. Some people appear to think that meditation is the only way there is to raise the level of consciousness, as if to say that consciousness must be raised directly by working on the mind itself or not at all. Such people therefore identify meditation with the spiritual life, and the spiritual life exclusively with meditation. They therefore claim that if you are not meditating you cannot possibly be leading a spiritual life. Sometimes they even identify the spiritual life with a particular kind of meditation, or a particular concentration technique. But this is far too narrow a view. It makes us forget what the spiritual life really is—which is to say that it consists in the raising of the level of consciousness—and it makes us forget, sometimes, what meditation itself really is. It is true, of course, that the raising of the level of consciousness by direct methods is at least as important as raising it by indirect methods; we might even say that it is perhaps more important. But we should not forget that other methods do exist; if we did forget this our approach would be too one-sided; and if we acted upon this, we would tend to make the spiritual life itself one-sided and even to exclude certain kinds of people—people of certain temperaments, for example—who were not, perhaps, particularly interested in meditation. So let us very briefly look at some of these indirect, non-meditative methods of raising the level of consciousness.

First of all there is change of environment. This is quite consciously employed as an indirect means of changing, and hopefully raising, our level of consciousness when we go away on retreat—perhaps into the country, to a retreat centre. There we spend a few days, or even a few weeks, simply in more pleasant, more congenial surroundings, perhaps not even doing anything in particular. This is often more helpful than people realize, and it suggests that the environment in which we normally have to live and work is not particularly good for us—does not help in the raising of the level of awareness. It really does seem as if, for most people, a positive change of environment leads quite naturally to a raising of their level of consciousness—even without any further effort.

Another quite practical and simple indirect method of raising the level of consciousness is what we call, in Buddhism, Right Livelihood. Practically everybody has to work for a living. Quite a lot of us do the same kind of work every day, five days a week, fifty weeks of the year. We may do it for five, ten, fifteen, twenty, twenty-five, or thirty years, until we come to the age of retirement. All this has a continuous effect on our state of mind. If our work is unhealthy in the mental, moral, and spiritual sense, the effect on our minds will also be unhealthy. So therefore, in Buddhism, in the Buddha's teaching, we are advised very strongly to look at our means of livelihood and to practise Right Livelihood, which means earning our living in a way which does not lower our state of consciousness, which does not prevent us raising it, even, and which does no harm to other living beings. In Buddhist tradition there is a list of occupations which are seen not to be very helpful: the work of a butcher, of a trader in arms, of a dealer in liquor, and so on. By changing our means of livelihood (assuming that at present it is not quite right), then just that change of work, change of place, change of environment—that change in the sort of people we work with, the sort of thing that we have to do every day—will have a positive and helpful effect on our level of consciousness—or at least it will not prevent it from rising.

Then again, to become more specific and concrete, there is the leading of a regular and disciplined life: something which apparently is becoming less and less popular. This may consist in the observance and practice of certain moral precepts and principles, in having regular hours for meals, for work, for recreation, and for study, or in observing moderation in such things as eating, sleeping, and talking—perhaps even in fasting occasionally, or observing silence for a few days or weeks. In its fully developed form this more regular, disciplined life is what we call the monastic life. Among those who are leading such a regular, disciplined life, even without any meditation, over a period of years, one can see quite clearly a change taking place in their state, their level, of consciousness.

There are other indirect methods, such as hatha yoga or yoga in the more physical sense. Especially there are what are called yogic *asanas*, which affect not only the body, but the mind as well. They affect the mind *through* the body, and even people who meditate regularly sometimes find these *asanas* very helpful. Sometimes even the experienced meditator may be a bit too tired at the end of a day's work, or a bit too worried, to meditate properly. At such times he may practise a few *asanas* until his mind becomes calmer and more concentrated. Thus he loses his tiredness and becomes more refreshed, almost as though he had meditated.

Then again there are the various Japanese *do* or 'ways'— like *ikebana*, flower arrangement. It might seem a very simple and ordinary thing, just to arrange a few flowers in a vase in a traditional way, but people who have engaged in this over a period of years are definitely changed in their minds, changed in their consciousness. One can also think of things like T'ai Chi Ch'uan and so on. These all have an effect upon the mind. They are all indirect ways of raising the level of consciousness. Likewise, the enjoyment of great works of art—of great poetry, music, and painting—often helps to raise the level of consciousness. Such enjoyment raises it if the works in question are truly great—if they really do issue from a higher state of consciousness in the artist himself—if they actually are an expression of a higher state of conscious-ness than we usually experience.

On a more practical level, there is simply helping other people. We might devote ourselves to helping the sick, the destitute, and the mentally disturbed, as well as to visiting those in prison. We might do these things very willingly and cheerfully, disregarding our own comfort and con-venience—might do them without any personal, selfish motive. This is what in the Hindu tradition is called *nishkama karma yoga*, or the yoga of disinterested action.

This too is an indirect means of raising our state of consciousness.

Then there is association with spiritually minded people, especially those who are more spiritually advanced than ourselves—if we are able to find them. Such association is regarded in some traditions, or by some teachers, as the most important of all the indirect methods. It is what is referred to again and again in Indian religious and spiritual literature as *satsangh*. *Sat* means true, real, authentic, genuine, spiritual—even transcendental—while *sangh* means association, or communion, or fellowship. *Satsangh* is simply a getting together—often in a very happy, carefree spirit—with people who are on the spiritual path and whose predominant interest is in spiritual things. This rubs off on oneself, almost without any effort on one's own part. Thus *satsangh* too is an indirect means of raising the level of consciousness. It is what in Buddhism we call *kalyana mitrata*.

Then again, there is chanting and ritual worship. Ritual is very much looked down upon today, especially by the more intelligent, or perhaps I should say 'intellectual'. But it is a time honoured method of raising the level of consciousness. Even if we simply offer a few flowers, or light a candle and place it in front of an image or picture, all this has an effect upon the mind, and sometimes we are surprised to find how much effect it does have. We might read lots of books about the spiritual life, we might even have tried to meditate—might even have succeeded in meditating—but sometimes we find that the performance of a simple, but meaningful, symbolic ritual action helps us far more.

There are many more indirect methods that could be mentioned, and these methods can of course be combined with each other. Some of them can be combined with the direct method, with the practice of meditation. However, good though these indirect methods are, some of them at least cannot carry us very far. They cannot carry us up through all the levels of consciousness. But since in most cases it will be quite a while before we do pass on to the higher levels of consciousness, the indirect methods will be useful to us for a long time. However, if by means of such methods we do succeed in getting anywhere near those higher levels then, in order to progress further, we shall have to have greater and greater recourse to meditation. We shall have to start working directly on the mind itself.

Now how do we do this? In what does this direct working on the mind consist? So far I have been using only the very general term 'meditation', because this is the one which has gained currency in the West, or at least in the English speaking countries. But this English word 'meditation' does not correspond to any one Indian or Buddhist term. What we call meditation in English corresponds to at least three rather different things, covers in fact three different ways of working directly on the mind—three different stages, even, in the development of consciousness—and for all these three things, Buddhism, like other Indian spiritual traditions, has quite separate terms. In plain English 'meditation' comprises Concentration, Absorption, and Insight.

THE STAGE OF CONCENTRATION

Concentration is of a twofold nature, involving both a narrowing of the focus of attention and a unification of energy. As such, concentration can be spoken of as integration, which is of two kinds, the 'horizontal' and the 'vertical' as I shall call them. Horizontal integration means the integration of the ordinary waking consciousness within itself, or on its own level, while vertical integration means the integration of the conscious mind with the subconscious mind, a process which involves the freeing of blocked somatic energy as well as the tapping of deeper and ever deeper energies within the psyche.

Horizontal integration corresponds to what is generally known as mindfulness and recollection. This English word 'recollection' is rather a good one, because it means just what it says—re-collection. It is a collecting together of what has been scattered, and what has been scattered is *ourselves*, our conscious selves, or so-called conscious selves. We have become divided into a number of selves, or part-selves, each with its own interests, its own desires, and so on, each trying to go its own way. At one time one self is uppermost, at another time another, so that sometimes we hardly know who we are. There is a dutiful self and there is a disobedient self. There is a self that would like to run away from it all, and there is a self that would like to stay at home and be a good boy, and so on. We hardly know, very often, which of these selves we really and truly are. Each of them is our self, and yet none of them is our self. The truth is that we do not really have a self at all. It has not yet come into existence. It has not yet been born. The self—the overall self, as it were—comes into existence only with the practice of mindfulness and recollection, when we 'collect' all these selves together.

Mindfulness, or recollection, in Buddhist tradition is of three kinds. Firstly, there is mindfulness of the body and its movements: knowing exactly where the body is and what it is doing. Here we make no unmindful movements, no movements of which we are unaware. When we speak, too, we are mindful, knowing what what we are saying and why we are saying it. We are fully alert, composed, aware. Secondly, there is mindfulness of feelings and emotions. We become quite clearly conscious of our passing, changing moods, of whether we are sad or happy, pleased or displeased, anxious, afraid, joyful, or excited. We watch, we see it all, we know exactly how we are. Of course this does not mean standing back from our feelings and emotions like a sort of spectator, looking at them in a very external, alienated way. It means experiencing our feelings and emotions—being 'with' them, not cut off from them—but at the same time being always mindful of them and observing them. Thirdly and lastly, there is mindfulness of thoughts: knowing just what we are thinking, just where our mind actually is from instant to instant. As we know, the mind wanders very easily. We are usually in an unconcentrated, unrecollected state as regards our thoughts. For this reason we have to practise being mindful of our thoughts, aware of what we are thinking from moment to moment.

If we practise in this way, then horizontal integration is achieved. We are brought together, and a self is created. When this is properly and perfectly done, we develop complete self consciousness: we become truly human. But concentration is not only horizontal; it is also vertical. The

conscious mind must now be integrated with the subconscious mind. This is achieved by having recourse to an
object of concentration—an object on which one learns to
concentrate one's whole attention, and into which the
energies of the subconscious are allowed to be gradually
absorbed.

At this point, the meditator, or the would-be meditator,
having achieved horizontal integration, has reached a
very crucial stage. He is about to make a very important
transition, from the plane or world of sensuous experience
to the plane or world of mental and spiritual form. But he
is held back by what are known as the five mental hindrances, which have to be suppressed before the stage of Absorption can be entered upon. (This suppression is
temporary. The five mental hindrances are permanently
eradicated only when Insight has been attained.) First of
all, there is the hindrance of desire for sensuous experience through the five physical senses, desire, that is,
for agreeable visual, auditory, olfactory, gustatory, and
tactile sensations—especially those connected with food
and with sex. So long as desires of this sort are present in
the mind, no transition to the stage of Absorption is possible, since while they are present the meditator cannot
really occupy himself with the concentration-object.
Secondly, there is the hindrance of hatred, which is the
feeling of ill will and resentment that arises when the
desire for sensuous experience is frustrated—a feeling that
is sometimes directed towards the object of the desire
itself. Thirdly comes the hindrance of sloth-and-torpor,
which keeps one on the plane of sensuous desire, on the
ordinary, everyday level of consciousness. It is a sort of
animal-like stagnation, both mental and physical.

Fourthly, there is the opposite hindrance to sloth-and-torpor, the hindrance of restlessness-and-worry. This is the inability to settle down to anything for very long. It is a state of continual fussing and bothering, never really getting anything done. Fifthly and lastly, there is the hindrance of doubt—not a sort of honest intellectual doubt, but something more like indecision, or even unwillingness to make up one's mind, to commit oneself. Basically, it is a lack of faith, a lack of trust: a reluctance to acknowledge that there is a higher state of consciousness for man to achieve. These, then, are the five mental hindrances which must be allowed to subside, or which must even be suppressed, before we take up the concentration-object and prepare to enter upon the stage of Absorption.

For a mind obscured by the five mental hindrances, as our minds so often are, there are five traditional similes, in each of which the mind itself is likened to water. The mind which is contaminated by desire for sensuous experience is likened to water in which various bright colours have been mixed. It is pretty, perhaps, but the purity and translucency of the water has been lost. The mind which is contaminated by hatred is, we are told, like water that has been brought to the boil, which is hissing and bubbling and seething. The mind contaminated by sloth-and-torpor is said to be like water choked with a thick growth of weeds, so that nothing can get through it. The mind contaminated by restlessness-and-worry is like water which has been whipped up into waves by the wind, even by a great storm. Lastly, the mind which is contaminated by doubt, by uncertainty, is like water full of mud. When the five hindrances are suppressed, the conscious mind becomes like pure water. It becomes cool, it becomes calm and clear. It is now ready to take up an object of concentration.

These objects of concentration, even in the Buddhist tradition alone, are of very many kinds. Some are rather ordinary and everyday, while others are rather extraordinary. First of all there is the breath, our own breath, as it comes in and goes out. There are various forms of this practice, several different techniques. Another object of concentration, a very important one, is sound, especially the sacred sound that we call *mantra*. Or we can take as an object of concentration a disc of very pure, bright colour, red or blue or green, etc., according to temperament. Again, we can make our object of concentration a piece of human bone, preferably a sizeable piece to provide a good solid object of concentration. Alternatively we can take an idea, take a concept of a particular virtue to be cultivated, such as generosity. And again—to take something quite ordinary and mundane—we can concentrate on the flame of a lamp, or on a candle. We can also concentrate on the various psychic centres within our own body, or on a mental image or picture of the Buddha, or of a great Bodhisattva or teacher. In all of these objects, whether the breath, the sound, the mantra, the flame, the image or picture of the Buddha, etc., the mind can become absorbed, even deeply absorbed.

We do not have to practise concentration with each and every one of these objects, though it is possible for several different concentration-objects to be combined in sequence in one particular system or tradition of meditation practice. The different objects of concentration can also be combined with some of the indirect methods of raising the level of consciousness, particularly, for example, with chanting and with ritual.

Now if we proceed in this manner, that is to say if we integrate the conscious mind with itself, if we integrate the conscious mind with the subconscious mind, if we suppress the five mental hindrances, if we take up an object or objects of concentration, and if our deeper energies start flowing more and more powerfully into the object of concentration, then a great change will take place: our level of consciousness definitely will start rising, from the plane or world of sensuous experience to the plane or world of mental and spiritual form. In other words, we begin to pass from the first to the second stage of meditation, from meditation in the sense of concentration to meditation in the sense of absorption.

THE STAGE OF ABSORPTION

Absorption, the second level of meditation, is generally divided into four levels, and throughout these four levels the process of vertical integration, begun at the stage of Concentration, continues. Here, it has to be noted, there is no question of integrating the conscious and the subconscious mind, for that has already been done. Here the purified, integrated conscious mind is itself integrated with the *superconscious*. And the energies of the superconscious—energies, that is to say, which are purely spiritual—begin to be tapped. Absorption represents, therefore, the unification of the mind on higher and ever higher levels of consciousness and being. As this process continues, our cruder mental states and cruder mental functions are progressively refined and our energies are absorbed into higher states and higher functions.

In what we call the first level of absorption there is a certain amount of mental activity present. We are still thinking about this and that, thinking, perhaps, subtle thoughts about worldly matters, or even thinking about our meditation practice itself. From the second level of absorption onwards, mental activity of this kind is entirely absent. Thinking as we know it entirely disappears. One might expect that because we are not thinking we should become dead and inert, but this would be a great mistake. We might even say that because we are *not* thinking, consciousness becomes clearer, brighter, more intense, more radiant than ever. But since thinking does not occur at the second and higher levels, it is important not to *think* about these levels of absorption too much, or preferably not at all. Instead, we should try to get some *feeling* of what they are like, proceeding not analytically, not intellectually, but with the help of images, symbols, and similes. We can best do this with the help of the four traditional similes for the four states of absorption—similes which go back to the Buddha's own personal teaching.

The simile for the first level of absorption is that of the soap powder and the water. The Buddha asks us to imagine that a bath-attendant takes some soap powder in one hand—apparently they had soap powder in ancient India—and some water in the other. He mixes the two together in a platter in such a way that all the water is fully absorbed by the soap powder, and all the soap powder thoroughly saturated by the water. There is not a single speck of soap powder unsaturated, and not a single drop of water left over. The first stage of absorption, the Buddha says, is just like that. In it, the entire psycho-physical organism is completely saturated with feelings of bliss, of ecstasy, of supreme happiness, and these feelings are all *contained*. At the same time, the whole being is *saturated*—there is no part of the being, physical or mental, un-saturated—and yet there is nothing left over. Thus there is no inequality, no imbalance. It is all calm, and steady, and stable, and firm: all naturally concentrated.

Describing the second level of absorption, the Buddha asks us to imagine a great lake of water, very pure, very calm and still. This lake is fed by a subterranean spring, so that all the time in the very heart of the lake there is a bubbling up of pure water from a very great depth. The second level of absorption is like this. It is calm and it is clear, it is peaceful, pure, translucent, but from an even greater depth there is something even *more* pure, even *more* bright, even *more* wonderful, bubbling up all the time. This 'something' is the higher spiritual element, the higher spiritual consciousness, by which we are now as it were infiltrated—by which we are inspired.

The third level of absorption, the Buddha says, is like the same lake, the same body of water, only with lotus blos-soms growing in it. These lotus blossoms are standing right in the water, are soaked and pervaded by it. They are thoroughly enjoying the water, you could say. Similarly, in the third level of absorption, we are, so to speak, bathing in that higher spiritual element, that higher spiritual con-sciousness—bathing in it and soaking in it, permeated by it within and surrounded by it without. This, the Buddha said, is what the third level of absorption is like.

In the case of the fourth and last level of absorption, the Buddha asks us to imagine a man who, on a very hot day, has a bath in a beautiful great tank of water. Having washed himself clean, he comes out, and then wraps his whole body in a sparklingly white, clean, new sheet—what Indians call a *dhoti*—so that he is swathed in it, and it completely covers and cloaks him. The fourth level of absorption, the Buddha says, is like that. We are insulated by that higher spiritual consciousness from the contact, and from the influence, of those states and levels which are lower. It is as though we were surrounded by a powerful aura. It is not that we immerse ourselves in that state, but rather that the state has descended into us, permeated us. Furthermore, it has started radiating outwards from us so that we have a sort of aura of meditation extending from us in all directions. In this state we cannot be easily influenced or easily affected, although we can easily influence and affect other people.

These, then, are the four levels of absorption. If we want to recall them, and get the *feeling* of them, perhaps we should just recollect the four beautiful similes given by the Buddha to illustrate them. Having traversed, at least in imagination, these four levels of absorption, we can now come on to the third and last stage of meditation.

THE STAGE OF INSIGHT

By Insight we mean the clear vision, the clear perception, of the true nature of things—of what in traditional Buddhist terminology is called things 'as they really are'. In other words, to use more abstract, more philosophical phraseology, it is a direct perception of Reality itself. This is what meditation at its height is—this is what Insight, or *sight*, really is. Such perception is twofold. It is insight into the conditioned, which is to say, the 'world', or whatever is mundane, transitory, and so on; and it is insight into the Unconditioned, that which transcends the world: the Absolute, the Ultimate.

The former, which is to say insight into the conditioned, consists in three things, or has three aspects. We see first of all that conditioned things, worldly things, by their very nature cannot give permanent and lasting satisfaction. For that we have to look elsewhere. Secondly, we see that all conditioned things are impermanent. We cannot possess any of them for ever. And thirdly and lastly, we see that all conditioned things are only relatively existent. They are not absolutely existent. They do not possess permanent, ultimate reality.

Now insight into the Unconditioned consists, in one formulation, of what are known as the Five Knowledges, or the Five Wisdoms. This is not knowledge in the ordinary sense, but something far beyond that. First of all there is what we can only describe as the knowledge of the totality of things, not so much in their aggregated particularity, but in and through their ultimate depths and spiritual essence—in the light of their common unifying principle. Then there is the knowledge of all things, conditioned and Unconditioned, without the slightest trace of subjective distortion. This knowledge is sometimes called the Mirror-Like Knowledge. It is so called because it is like a great mirror which reflects everything just as it is— without subjectivity, or prejudice, or dimming, or clouding, or obscuration. In it everything is seen just as it is. Thirdly, there is the knowledge of things in their absolute sameness and identity—seeing everywhere one mind, one Reality, one *shunyata*. Fourthly, there is the knowledge of things in their difference. The absolute unity does not wipe out the absolute difference. There is no one-sidedness. We see things in their absolute unity, but we also see them in their absolute multiplicity—their absolute uniqueness. We see them in both ways at once. And then, finally, there is the knowledge of what is to be done for the spiritual welfare of other living beings.

These Five Knowledges, or Five Wisdoms, are symbolized in Buddhist iconography by what we call the Mandala of the Five Buddhas. Visualizing this Mandala, we see first of all a vast expanse of blue sky, very deep and very brilliant. At the centre of this expanse we see appearing a pure white Buddha figure, holding in his hand a brilliant golden wheel. Then in the east we see a deep, dark blue Buddha holding in his hand a 'diamond sceptre'. In the south we see a golden yellow Buddha holding in his hand a brilliantly shining jewel. In the west we see a deep red Buddha holding in his hand a red lotus. And in the north we see a green Buddha, holding two 'diamond sceptres' crossed.

When all the Five Knowledges dawn, Enlightenment has been attained. We become, ourself, the embodiment of all five Buddhas. At this stage Insight has been fully developed, meditation has been practised to the very limit, and we have understood for ourselves what meditation really is.

The Meaning of Spiritual Community

IN THE FIRST of these three lectures I dealt with a very lofty subject, with nothing less than the Ideal of Human Enlightenment itself. In the second lecture I dealt, in part at least, with quite advanced, quite sublime, spiritual experiences, such as might not come to everybody—at least not for a while. But in this lecture I'm going to deal with something very down to earth, something that could be of personal and practical significance for anyone: The Meaning of Spiritual Community. I shall deal with the subject under three main headings: Who are the members of the Spiritual Community? Where is the Spiritual Community to be found? And, What do the members of the Spiritual Community do—for themselves, for one another, and even for the world?

However, before taking up the first of these questions, I would like to resolve a possible misunderstanding about the word 'spiritual'. We speak of the *spiritual* community, the *spiritual* life, the *spiritual* ideal, and *spiritual* practice; but the question arises, what do we mean by the word 'spiritual'? It is a word that we very often use, perhaps in quite a number of different senses. Sometimes people use the word rather loosely, and sometimes, I am afraid, people use it in no sense at all, but rather to disguise general poverty of thought, or to convey a vague sense of uplift. It is therefore important that we clarify the meaning of this word.

In my own usage of the term, as you will have seen from these lectures, the 'spiritual' is to be contrasted with the 'psychological', as well as with what I call the 'worldly'. By 'psychological' I mean consisting of, or pertaining to, mental states, including mental processes or functions, *in general*; and by 'spiritual' I mean consisting of, or pertaining to, what are called *skilful* mental states.

Now this in turn raises the question of what is meant by the word skilful. After all, this is a term that we come across again and again in Buddhist literature. In fact, this word 'skilful', with its antonym 'unskilful', is one of the most important terms in the whole range of Buddhist psychology and ethics. Unskilful means consisting of, or associated with, craving, aversion, and delusion, while skilful, on the contrary, means consisting of, or associated with, the absence of these states, that is to say, with the absence of craving, aversion, and delusion. Putting it more positively, skilful mental states are those associated with content (one might almost say peace of mind), friendliness, and knowledge—in the sense of wisdom.

You may have noticed that Buddhist literature does not speak in terms of good and evil. It does not use terms like sin, or vice, or virtue—at least not in their Christian sense. When it is speaking precisely and accurately—speaking as it were philosophically—in its own distinctive language, it speaks in terms of what is skilful and what is unskilful. Such usage suggests quite a number of things. It suggests, for instance, that good intentions or good feelings are not enough. It suggests that what we call the 'good' life must include an element of knowledge, of *understanding*. We therefore find that, in Buddhist literature, there is no such thing as the 'holy fool', which is to say, someone who is good, even very good, but stupid. For Buddhism this would be a contradiction in terms. The Buddhist usage of the term skilful also suggests that by being *un*skilful we get ourselves into difficulties—even incur inconvenience, not to say suffering—just as if we handle a knife or chisel clumsily, then sooner or later we are bound to cut ourselves.

The three English words craving, aversion, and delusion, do render quite faithfully and accurately, indeed almost literally, the three corresponding terms in the original languages, Sanskrit and Pali, but perhaps they do not give us much real insight into the meaning of those terms. A Tibetan source, however, gives a more extended and detailed account. According to this source, craving is 'longing desire to possess objects of sensuous cognition which you like, and to include them in your ego-identity, in the hope of getting a sense of security from "having them as part of you".' Aversion is defined as 'fearful and angered repulsion to get rid of objects of sensuous cognition which you dislike, and to exclude them from your ego-identity, in the hope of getting a sense of security from "not having them as part of you".' As you can see from these definitions, one is the opposite of the other. Finally, delusion, which is defined as 'a stubborn closed-mindedness about learning anything which you feel might threaten your ego-identity, and upset the sense of security you wish to get from it, but which you are unaware of, and therefore feel you must protect'. Even though comparatively short, these three definitions are quite profound and far-reaching.

With the help of these three definitions we can begin to see what is meant by Spiritual Community. By Spiritual Community we mean a community which encourages the development in its members of skilful, rather than unskilful, mental states as being the best ideal for human beings. In the same way, the spiritual life is a life devoted to the elimination of unskilful, and to the development of skilful, mental states. In a higher sense, it is a life which is based entirely upon, and is expressive of, the skilful mental states of contentment or peace of mind, friendliness, and wisdom. Spiritual practice, it follows, is therefore any observance, any method or exercise, which is conducive to the eradication of unskilful, and to the development of skilful, mental states.

The distinction between skilful and unskilful mental states can serve as a basis for distinguishing between different levels of experience. Firstly, there is a level of consciousness on which only unskilful mental states are present, secondly, there is a level of consciousness on which only skilful mental states are present, and thirdly, there is a level of consciousness which is just mixed. Further, these three levels of consciousness can be seen to correspond with three planes of existence. Arranging them in a slightly different way, in an ascending order, we get, first of all, what we may call the *worldly plane*. This is a plane of existence on which people are motivated entirely, or almost entirely, by the unskilful thoughts of craving, aversion, and delusion. It is a 'state' in which they perform unskilful acts, which is to say: they harm other living beings, take what has not been given, and indulge in sexual misconduct. They also speak unskilful words: words which are untrue or false, which are harsh and malicious, which create dissension, and which are idle, frivolous, and useless. This, then, is the worldly plane, or plane of worldly life. We could simply call it *the world*.

The mixed plane is a plane of struggle, of effort and contest. It is a plane on which skilful and unskilful states are fairly evenly balanced. It is the plane where we find those who have just started to lead a spiritual life, who have just started trying to evolve. Just as an amphibian is a creature which lives partly in the water and partly on dry land, so the person dwelling on this mixed plane is spiritually amphibious. Sometimes such a person is very worldly, but at other times he might be quite spiritual.

Thirdly, there is the *spiritual plane*. This is the plane on which people are motivated entirely, or almost entirely, by skilful mental states: motivated by contentment, love, and knowledge; motivated by mindfulness, energy, faith, joy, compassion, and so on. It is the plane on which they perform actions that are helpful, generous, and pure, where they speak words that are true, that are affectionate, that promote concord and harmony, and that conduce to the good of the hearer.

As you will have seen in the previous lecture, Buddhism speaks in terms of four levels of consciousness: consciousness associated with the plane of sensuous experience, consciousness associated with the plane of mental and spiritual form, consciousness associated with the formless plane, and, finally, consciousness associated with the transcendental path and with nirvana. What I am here calling the *world* therefore corresponds with the plane of sensuous experience, and what I am here calling the spiritual plane corresponds with the plane of mental and spiritual form, together with the formless plane. Sometimes the word 'spiritual' is used in such a way as to include the transcendental as well, but my own preference is to make quite a sharp distinction between the spiritual and the transcendental.

It is perhaps worth noting here that the spiritual plane corresponds to meditation in the sense of absorption. It therefore follows that the meditation experience is best seen as being an uninterrupted flow of skilful mental states, without any unskilful thought intruding. This is what meditation essentially is, and this is quite a useful way of looking at it, since it makes it clear that meditation does not necessarily mean *sitting* in meditation. Meditation, essentially, is simply this flow of spiritual thoughts— whether we are sitting, walking, standing, or doing anything else.

If living in the world means being motivated by unskilful thoughts, speaking unskilful words, and performing unskilful actions, and if the spiritual life consists in the progressive eradication of unskilful, and the development of skilful, mental states—consists eventually in being entirely motivated by such states—then the more we lead a spiritual life the less we will tend to live in the world. This separation, this leaving the world behind, may be only mental, but it may be physical as well. People sometimes say that it is enough to give something up mentally, and that to do it physically and verbally is not so important. Usually, however, we do not really know whether or not we have given something up unless we try to do it literally. In Buddhism the literal giving up of the world is traditionally known as 'the going forth from home into the homeless life'. Essentially, it consists in giving up worldly attitudes, giving up unskilful mental states. But it is not easy to do this, especially if the people all around you are freely indulging in such states and giving expression to them in the form of unskilful words and unskilful deeds, and even expecting *you* to join in. In this way a great deal of strain and tension arises, even a great deal of conflict. *You* are trying to do one thing, *they* are trying to do another. *You* are trying to develop skilful thoughts, *they* are giving way to unskilful thoughts. One day—or one night—you decide that you cannot stand the strain any longer. You just want to be free: free from that struggle, that conflict. You want to be free to stand on your own feet, free to develop in your own way, *skilfully*. So you just give up everything. You just walk out. You *go forth*.

We have, in the Buddhist tradition, a classic example of this Going Forth in the story of the Buddha himself—or rather of the future Buddha, the Buddha-to-be. If you know, at least in outline, the story of the Buddha, you will know that Siddhartha, as he then was, was born into the proud and warlike Shakya tribe. Coming from a wealthy and aristocratic family, he was in the position of being able to satisfy whatever desires he had. Whether health, youth, strength, riches, social position, or education, he had everything that the world could offer. He had plenty of leisure, plenty of friends and relations; he had a wife and a child. But although he had all these things, they could not give him what he really wanted. For even though he may not have known it at this stage, what he really wanted was something spiritual, something transcendental. He consequently felt worldly life to be increasingly oppressive, increasingly stuffy, and, one day, he decided to leave it all.

He waited until nightfall, until everybody was asleep, and then rode out into the night on his favourite horse, leaving behind his palace, leaving his home, accompanied, we are told, by a single faithful servant, who ran along at the heels of the horse. He rode until dawn broke, when he found himself on the bank of a river which marked the boundary of his father's territory. He then dismounted, cut off his hair and beard with his sword, and then exchanged clothes with a beggar who happened to be passing by. Finally, he sent the horse and the servant home, and went on his way alone. This is known as the 'Going Forth' of Siddhartha, who became the Buddha. It is also known as the 'Great Renunciation', and for Buddhists it is the classic example of Going Forth—of Going Forth not just mentally but literally, with *body, speech,* and mind. One could even say that the Buddha's Going Forth is the archetypal Going Forth. After all, it is not only Siddhartha who has Gone Forth. Many people have Gone Forth, not just in the Buddha's day but in all ages of history; not just in the past, but also in the present. Perhaps, by virtue of the fact that you are listening to this lecture, you too have Gone Forth—not literally perhaps, but certainly mentally to some extent: Gone Forth from at least some worldly attitudes, from conventional ways of thinking, and from collective attitudes of various kinds.

But what happens when we have Gone Forth? Very often, of course, nothing happens. Very often we just continue to Go Forth, indefinitely as it were, and remain on our own. If we are 'lucky', however, something does happen: we start to meet others who have Gone Forth in the same sort of way as ourselves. Moreover, we meet not only people who have 'gone forth' *from* but people who have 'gone forth' *to*: people who are committed to the spiritual, committed, even, to the transcendental. In other words, we have come in contact with the Spiritual Community.

You may be thinking by now that it has taken us a long time to get around to the Spiritual Community! But this is, in fact, what very often happens. Siddhartha himself, the future Buddha, never came in contact with the Spiritual Community—not, at least, during his period of Going Forth. He had to establish one after his Enlightenment. But we are much more fortunate. We do have the opportunity of coming into contact with the Spiritual Community. What is it, then, that we come into contact with?

WHO ARE THE MEMBERS OF THE SPIRITUAL COMMUNITY?

In brief, we may say that the members of the Spiritual Community are individuals who have gone for Refuge. They are individuals who have committed themselves to what are known as the 'Three Jewels'. Before saying more about the Three Jewels, however, I would like first of all to draw attention to this word 'individual'. In consisting of individuals, the Spiritual Community consists of people who have made an individual choice and an individual decision. They have accepted responsibility for their own lives, and have decided that they want to develop as human beings, want to grow. The Spiritual Community is not, therefore, a group in the ordinary sense. It is not something collective, with a collective mind or soul. It has no collective identity in which you lose your own, or in which you become submerged. The Spiritual Community is a voluntary association of free individuals who have come together on account of a common commitment to a common ideal: a commitment to what we call the Three Jewels.

The Three Jewels are, firstly, the Ideal of Human Enlightenment, secondly, the Path of the Higher Evolution—which is to say, the Path of successively higher levels of consciousness, from self consciousness to absolute consciousness—and thirdly, the Spiritual Community itself. The Spiritual Community consists, therefore, of all those who, with the object of attaining Enlightenment, are devoting themselves to the development of skilful, rather than unskilful, mental states. In the highest sense, the third Jewel is what we call the transcendental community: it is that part of the Spiritual Community which has not only gone for Refuge, not only developed skilful mental states—not only become *absorbed*—but which has developed Insight: which sees, at least for a moment, Reality—face to face. Members of this 'community' have broken the first three fetters, as they are called, which bind man to conditioned existence. They are prepared to die in order that they may be spiritually reborn. Their practice of the Path is wholehearted, and not merely conventional. Their commitment is absolute, without any reservations whatsoever.

In more traditional Buddhist language, the Three Jewels are known as the Buddha-Jewel, the Dharma-Jewel, and the Sangha-Jewel. They are called jewels because, until modern times, jewels were the most precious of all material things. So the Three Jewels represent, in the same way, what is spiritually most precious, spiritually most valuable, and spiritually most worthwhile. In short they represent the highest values of, and for, human existence.

In more concrete terms, the members of the Spiritual Community are all those who have been 'ordained'—to use the English word in a very provisional sense. They have committed themselves to the Three Jewels not just mentally, but fully and openly, with body and speech as well: they have committed themselves with their whole being. Further, that commitment has been acknowledged by existing members of the Spiritual Community, in particular by a senior member of the Community. They have also pledged themselves to the observance of certain moral precepts. Members of the Spiritual Community, in this sense, may be young or old, male or female, 'educated' or uneducated. They may be living at home with their family—living, that is to say, outwardly in the world—or they may have 'gone forth' in the literal sense. They may be lay brothers or lay sisters, as they are sometimes called, or they may be monks or nuns—to use rather un-Buddhistic expressions. They may be more, or less, spiritually advanced. But *all* have gone for Refuge, all are committed to the Three Jewels, and are therefore all, equally, members of the Spiritual Community.

WHERE IS THE SPIRITUAL COMMUNITY TO BE FOUND?

The Spiritual Community is to be found wherever there are individuals who have gone for Refuge. Especially, it is found wherever such individuals are in personal contact, where they meet regularly. Of course, that contact is not simply social: it is spiritual, one might even say existential.

Where members of the Spiritual Community live under the same roof they are known as a residential Spiritual Community. Residential spiritual communities can be of various kinds. For instance, they can be monastic—or semi-monastic—in character. (I do not particularly like the word 'monastic', which is not a very Buddhistic expression, but we do not seem to have a better one in the English language.) The monastic—or semi-monastic—residential spiritual community can be a community of men or a community of women. In either case, the members of the community live together under comparatively ideal conditions, often in a quiet, secluded place, and they devote themselves mainly to study, to meditation, and to productive work—the last usually taking a 'co-operative' form.

In some parts of the Buddhist world, the Spiritual Community has come to be identified exclusively with the monastic community—even with the monastic community in a rather formalistic sense. This, however, is a great mistake. The Spiritual Community consists of all those who have gone for Refuge.

WHAT DO THE MEMBERS OF THE SPIRITUAL COMMUNITY DO— FOR THEMSELVES, FOR ONE ANOTHER, AND FOR THE WORLD?

Firstly, what do they do for themselves? Clearly, they carry on with their individual spiritual practice. They continue to study, they meditate, they practise Right Livelihood, they observe the precepts, and so on. But this is rather general. To explain, however, what members of the Spiritual Community do for themselves *as* members of the Spiritual Community, is very difficult, since it means describing, to some extent at least, what it is like to *be* a member of the Spiritual Community. It is possible to say one thing, however. A member of the Spiritual Community puts himself, or herself, in a position of being able to relate to others on a purely spiritual basis, or at least on a predominantly spiritual basis: on the basis of a common spiritual ideal, a common spiritual commitment.

Now what does this mean? We meet people all the time, whether at home, at a club, in a coffee bar, or wherever, and we relate to these people that we meet in a number of different ways. Usually, we relate on the basis of our own need—though the need may, of course, be mutual. Sometimes it is a sexual need, sometimes it is an economic need or a social need, but it is a need, and the relationship is therefore very often exploitive, even mutually exploitive. Of course, we do not usually care to admit this—do not care to say what it is that we really want from other people. Sometimes we do not even fully and consciously know what we are really looking for ourselves. This means that only too often our relationships are dishonest or, at best, confused. It means that they are accompanied by a certain amount of mutual misunderstanding, and a certain amount of rationalization.

Within the Spiritual Community, however, we do not relate to others in this kind of way. Within the Spiritual Community the situation is that we all want to develop spiritually. After all, we have all gone for Refuge! We therefore relate on the basis of our common commitment and our common ideal—relate on the basis of our highest common interest, our highest common concern. If, moreover, we relate to others on this basis, then we experience others in a way in which we do not usually experience them. We experience them as spiritual beings.

And because we experience *others* as spiritual beings—because we are *relating* to them as spiritual beings—we experience *ourselves* as spiritual beings too. In this way the pace of spiritual development is accelerated. We experience ourselves more and more truly, more and more intensely. Within the Spiritual Community, then, we can be ourselves as we are at our best and at our highest. Very often, when we speak of 'being ourselves', we mean being ourselves at our worst, letting out that part of ourselves that we do not usually like to acknowledge. But there is another way in which we can be ourselves, for, very often, it is the best in us, rather than the worst, that has no opportunity to express itself. So, within the context of the Spiritual Community, we can be ourselves at our best. If necessary, we can be ourselves at our 'worst' occasionally, but the important thing is that we can *be ourselves* fully, wholly, and perfectly.

To be ourselves in this way is rarely possible within the context of ordinary life, even with our 'nearest and dearest', whether parents, husbands or wives, or our closest friends. Only too often, on certain occasions, or in connection with certain topics, we cannot be fully ourselves—not even with one person. Indeed, quite a few people go through their lives without being able to be themselves completely and continuously with anyone. They consequently find it very difficult even to *experience* themselves as they are, even to experience themselves at their best.

Within the Spiritual Community, on the other hand, we can be ourselves, and not just with one person, but even with two or three people—even with many people. This sort of experience is, perhaps, unprecedented in the lives of the majority of people. Just imagine, for a moment, what it would be like if you were to have five or six—or even fifty or sixty—people present, but all of you *being yourselves*. This should be quite possible within the Spiritual Community, because here we are relating on the basis of the shared spiritual commitment, the shared spiritual ideal—relating on the basis of what is best and highest in each and every one of us. We therefore experience, within the Spiritual Community, a great relief and a great joy. There is no need to put up any psychological defences, no need to pretend, no need to guard against misunderstanding. With complete transparency we can be ourselves with others who are also being themselves.

In a situation like this, we naturally develop more rapidly than would otherwise be possible. We do a great deal for ourselves simply by being members of the Spiritual Community—that is to say, *active* members, though really there is no other kind.

What do members of the Spiritual Community also do for one another? Obviously they help one another in all possible ways—*not* just spiritually. They help one another psychologically, economically, and even in quite simple, everyday matters. However, I am going to mention two ways in which members of the Spiritual Community help one another which are particularly relevant. As I have said, within the Spiritual Community we relate on the basis of the common spiritual commitment, the common spiritual ideal. But this is not always easy. After all, many people 'join' the Spiritual Community: many people commit themselves. Among them there are people of many different kinds, having different backgrounds, different outlooks, different temperaments. We may find some of them quite easy to get on with, and others not so easy. We may find some of them impossible to get on with! So what are we to do? We do not want to leave the Spiritual Community, and we can hardly ask *them* to leave. There is only one thing for us to do: to work hard on it together. We have to recognize that what we have in common is much more important than what we do not have in common. We have to learn to relate—even painfully learn—on the basis of that which we do have in common. This certainly is not easy, but with patience we can gradually succeed. In this way, members of the Spiritual Community help one another—help one another to overcome purely subjective, purely personal limitations and learn how to relate on the basis of what is higher.

Again, spiritual life is not easy. It is not easy to eradicate unskilful thoughts, not easy to develop skilful ones. Sometimes we may feel like giving up altogether. 'It's too much for us, it goes too much against the grain, there are too many difficulties,' we may protest. We may even think of leaving the Spiritual Community. At times like these, members of the Spiritual Community help one another: support one another, encourage one another, inspire one another. This is the most important thing that they can do for one another, perhaps, this bearing one another up when they get into a difficult and disturbed condition, or when they get depressed, as any member of the Spiritual Community may until such time as he has his feet firmly on the Path. When going through this kind of crisis, it is a great comfort, a great consolation, to have around us others who sincerely wish us well, who desire our spiritual welfare, and who can help us through this quite difficult period.

Finally, what do members of the Spiritual Community do for the world? You might expect me to say here something about the role of the Spiritual Community in world history, or its significance for the total evolutionary process, but such considerations would take us beyond the scope of this brief exposition. I shall confine myself, instead, to a few practical points, and then conclude.

First of all, there is one thing that needs to be made clear. Members of the Spiritual Community are not obliged to do anything at all for the world, the operative word here being *obliged*. Whatever they do, they do quite freely: they do it because they want to, because they like doing it. There is no obligation involved. They do it, even, as part of the process of their own spiritual development, their own spiritual life. To put this in a slightly different way, the Spiritual Community does not have to justify its existence to the world. It does not have to show that it brings about social and economic improvements, that it is helpful to the government or the administration. It does not have to show that it benefits the world *in a worldly sense*.

However, in general, the members of the Spiritual Community do two things for the world. First of all, they keep the Spiritual Community itself in existence. One might say that it is good for the world that such a thing as the Spiritual Community should simply be there, good that there should be people around who are dedicated to the spiritual life, dedicated to the development of skilful states of mind. This is good because it helps to develop a more wholesome atmosphere in the world.

Secondly, members of the Spiritual Community help the world by building a bridge between the world and the Spiritual Community—or at least laying down a few stepping-stones. They do this by getting together, in teams of four, or five, or more, and conducting various activities conducive to the development of skilful mental states. These activities help people to evolve from the worldly plane to the mixed plane, perhaps even from the mixed plane to the spiritual plane. These activities might be meditation classes, retreats, lectures, yoga classes, courses in human communication, and so on. They are open to anyone who cares to take advantage of them: one does not even have to join anything, or pay a subscription!

In this way members of the Spiritual Community, or those individuals who are committed to the Ideal of Human Enlightenment—committed to the attainment of higher levels of consciousness and insight—help people in the world to develop more and more skilful thoughts, to grow in contentment, in love, and in understanding, and to know indeed, for themselves, the meaning of Spiritual Community.

ALSO FROM WINDHORSE

KAMALASHILA

MEDITATION :

THE BUDDHIST WAY OF TRANQUILLITY AND INSIGHT

A comprehensive guide to the methods and theory of meditation giving basic
techniques for the beginner and detailed advice for the more experienced
meditator. A practical handbook firmly grounded in Buddhist tradition but readily
accessible to people with a modern Western background.

288 pages, 244 x 175, with charts and illustrations
ISBN 0 904766 56 X
Paperback £11.99 / $22.99

For orders and catalogues, contact

WINDHORSE PUBLICATIONS

3 SANDA STREET

GLASGOW G20 8PU

SCOTLAND